Bar/Bat Mitzvah
The Complete
Planning Guide

By J. Hilton Dies

A Newbiz Playbook Publication

FIRST EDITION

For downloadable tools emailed directly to you please email products@newbizplaybook.com use the password bar/bat in the re: of the email

For my family, the answer to my why

How to Use this Book

I wrote this book because of widespread demand from consumers of some of my other work on Wedding and Event Planning. I got special requests from grandmothers who wanted to plan a bar/bat mitzvah for a grandchild, and from elite planners who lacked the proper perspective or familiarity with Jewish tradition and custom to provide their clients with the level of service they wanted to achieve.

This book is meant to serve both. Not all chapters will be helpful to all audiences, but this book has been designed to contain everything you might need to successfully plan one of these events.

There are a number of tools contained in these pages, and I am happy to make all of them available to you in electronic form so that you may customize them to meet your personal or business needs.

Much of the information contained here will spill over into other kinds of event planning, including sections on interviewing venues, photographers etc., but the hope is that ultimately you will feel that you received value well in excess of what you paid for this book.

To receive the electronic tools contained herein, please email us at **products@newbizplaybook.com** use the password Bar/Bat in the re: of the email.

Enjoy!

Understanding Your "Product"

Whether you are doing it for family, or for hire the fundamental truth about Bar/Bat Mitzvah planning is that the product is meant to be a dream that celebrates the traditional passage into adulthood for a beloved child. Many of the people looking for your expertise have imagined this moment for their children, from the time they were born. Your task is to deliver that perfect day. One of the biggest mistakes that new planners make is to try to use low prices, or the perception of discounted value to attract customers. If you are planning the event for your own family, you want it to run smoothly and be a joy filled event for friends and family. If you are doing it for hire, your customers don't want the cheap option, and what's more they will be less likely to hire someone offering it.

People who hire professionals for this service are looking for an elite experience, for you that means incredible responsiveness. You provide a cell phone. You answer emails within hours if not minutes. For that your customers will pay a premium. Your image, dress, tone, and interactions create this experience.

Nordstrom's is not an inexpensive store. Their products are expensive, even more expensive than other stores by a fair margin, but their client service and return policies are exceptional. The Ritz Carlton hosts very nice facilities, but honestly for the cost, they are not materially better than many less expensive hotels. The difference is in service, and the way they make their patrons feel.

Ignore this fundamental truth, and none of these contents will matter. Embrace it, and you will succeed. The goal is to create Raving Fans at every opportunity. The clients you help will have friends and family getting married, and you want them to insist on you to handle them.

Cost Projections

One of the first questions you will have or get from those who hire you is how to plan for costs of a Bar/Bat Mitzvah.

The following is meant to be a guideline. Keep in mind that if you are planning this event for hire, you may be charging by the hour ($75-$350 per hour is not uncommon), as a percentage of the cost of the event (10-20% is the typical range here), or if you have the venue and are hosting in your own location, you may simply charge a total price. This will impact client costs, and should be taken into consideration.

Invitations will range from 1-5 dollars depending on whether they are custom printed, design used and quantity ordered

Catering ranges from a low of $15 dollars per adult to more than $100 depending upon the food, whether the venue is included, and the number of people. This would not include a high end tiered cake, which will cost between $1-3 dollars per slice.

Venues can vary widely nationwide, and even in particular areas, depending on peak times. Expect to pay between $500 and $2500 for most venues, and with a larger group that number can get much higher.

Entertainment Costs are as follows:

DJ $500 - $1500 depending upon the amount of time, and whether additional light packages, extra sound equipment (such as karaoke), etc. are requested. DJ's are recommended for most parties as bands may have less ability to entertain the group which is very likely to be quite diverse at these events.

Magicians, and other party hosts that provide party or arcade games usually start in the $400 range and go up depending upon the request. Given that young children are very often in attendance at these events, balloon animals and other forms of entertainment may be popular.

Donations for the Rabbi(s) and Cantor – Different temples will vary, and some will have a Bar Mitzvah fee for hosting the celebration. It is common for such donations to be given to the Rabbi's discretionary fund. Some donors give in increments of 18 the multiple of chai, though it is not required. These donations are a function of the personal circumstances of the family however they are approached.

Extras

Flowers – These range from simple arrangements that can be obtained for less than $500, to more elaborate decorations that rival the cost of weddings in the $2000-$4000 range.

Gifts for attendees – They can be thoughtful photo packages of the child, which are less expensive, or t-shirts and more that add up. These are absolutely a function of your preference.

Manicures, Pedicures, Hair and Makeup – Don't ignore these as they will add up during your Bat Mitzvah.

Very often activities will be planned that also double as gifts for the kids in attendance. Examples of these include photo booths, candy making bars, wax hands, design your own flip flops etc.,

Industry estimates show that typical Bar/Bat Mitzvah's cost between $15,000 and $30,000 dollars, but these numbers are skewed as many families choose to host their own events, and privately subcontract catering etc., which wouldn't involve the "industry," much at all.

We have attached a simple budget tool here, but can send an electronic version upon request to products@newbizplaybook.com

Service or Vendor	Estimated Cost	Actual Cost	Deposit Due	Balance Due
Banquet Hall				
Caterer & Bar				
DJ/Band				
Photography				
Videography				
Decorations				
Invitations/Postage				
Entertainment				
Florist				
Event Planner				
Favors & Gifts				
Judaica				
Clothing				
Cake				
Friday Night Oneg Shabbat				
Saturday Kiddush Luncheon				
Personal Expenses				
Rental Items				
Transportation				
Morning After Brunch				
Synagogue Fees/Officiant Fees				
Total	$0.00	$0.00		$0.00

Bar/Bat Mitzvah Planning Checklist

The following is meant to be fully inclusive. There are likely to be items that you do not need or want, or that are not in your budget for the event you are planning. Your Synagogue or Temple may also have varying requirements related to education expectations for the child and family. Be sure to look into these as early as possible. If you are planning an event for hire, be sure to involve the family in making sure these things get handled. It is not uncommon for families to be so caught up in the celebration aspect of this event, that they become distracted by the more serious religious implications that are involved. No one wants to ruin this special time by finding out that the Synagogue or Temple, or the Rabbi or Cantor is unwilling or unable to assist, because all items were not handled.

2+ Years Before the Bar/Bat Mitzvah

- Get Dates from the Synagogue or Temple
- Plan High Level Details of Event Budget etc.
- Start Building Excitement in Your Child

1+ Year Before the Bar/Bat Mitzvah

- Book Venue
- Consider options for Mitzvah projects
- Book Photographer or Videographer
- Determine the torah and haftorah portion and Confirm with your Rabbi
- Meet the Rabbi or Cantor to discuss the b'nai mitzvah process
- Hire Event Planner
- Consider catering, DJ's and Entertainment

- Begin to Formalize themes

6 – 12 Months Before the Bar/Bat Mitzvah

- Attend Shabbat Services as a family
- Select invitations, and make floral arrangements
- Buy Tallit and Tefillin if needed
- Block rooms for out of town guests at a desirable hotel
- Finalize themes with your child
- Order favors
- Order yarmulkes
- Confirm timeline, requirements, and educational expectations for your child with Rabbi and/or Cantor, and Synagogue or Temple
- Start Mitzvah Project
- Finalize guest list
- Order invitations
- Plan other events as needed (Shabbat Kiddush/Dinner, Sunday Brunch)
- Book DJ/Entertainment

2-5 Months Before the Bar/Bat Mitzvah

- Make Hotel Package with addresses, phone numbers and details for out of town guests
- Confirm rentals if renting tents, tables, chairs, chair covers etc.,
- Get invitations completed and assembled.
- Bar/Bat Mitzvah begins writing the dvar torah
- Make transportation arrangements as needed for guests with no cars, or elderly who cannot drive
- Submit photos for a video montage set to music to play at the party if desired
- Make Hair and makeup appointments

- Order cake or deserts if not provided by caterer

1-2 Months Before the Bar/Bat Mitzvah

- Mail the invitations
- Submit music preferences or special songs to DJ
- Compose Poems and candle lighting intros
- Bar/Bat Mitzvah prepares welcome/thank you speech
- Pay for flowers, photographers, and provide deposits as required
- Consider choices for Aliyot and honors
- Finalize ceremony program
- Consider choices for candle lighting
- Finalize seating arrangements
- Bar/Bat Mitzvah finalizes the dvar torah,
- Buy or put together gifts received book for thank you letters and memories
- Purchase items not provided by caterer (Kiddush cups, challah knife, etc.)

2-4 Weeks Before the Bar/Bat Mitzvah

- Finalize Aliyot and Honors
- Finalize Candle lighters
- Order food for Kiddush or Oneg Shabbat
- Pay Synagogue fees
- Confirm head counts
- Finalize prayers, speeches, and poems
- Confirm dates and details with photographer florist and pay deposits as required – provide special requests for family photos to be taken
- Provide final head counts to venue and caterer.

1 Week Before the Bar/Bat Mitzvah

- ○ Confirm brunch arrangements
- ○ Confirm hair and makeup appointments
- ○ Make final payments to vendors
- ○ Finalize seating chart
- ○ Have a rehearsal at the Synagogue or Temple

Venue Checklist

This checklist is to be used for interviewing venues, and tracking their answers to insure that they are a good fit for your or the client's needs. It is always a good idea to tour the venue early where economics permit, to see for yourself if the place is as nice as the well situated online pictures make it appear to be. When a venue impresses you, be sure to document that, and keep it mind. Relationships with quality reliable vendors are absolutely essential to success in this business.

Capacity

_____ Invited Guest Capacity
_____ Reception Area
_____ Theatre/Meeting Room
_____ Dining Area

Caterer

_____ Exclusive caterers?
_____ In-house tables/linens/chairs? If so, check out the quality.
_____ Typical menu cost per head for cocktails, heavy appetizers, etc.
_____ Bar tender charges?
_____ Serving Charges?
_____ Cake cutting charges?
_____ Minimum food and beverage spend?
_____ How early can your caterer arrive day of event to set up?

Rental Fees

_____ Usually negotiable, especially for a major brand/off day

_____ Does fee include a set up day?

_____ How early/late can your teams load in?

_____ Any discount for payment by check or early payment?

_____ Hotels should waive any room rentals when F&B meets a min.

Bathrooms

_____ Will you need to provide extra amenities to make the room nicer

_____ Cleanliness – poorly kept restrooms reflect poorly managed venue

_____ Number of stalls vs. number of guests

Parking

_____ Existent?

_____ Fee to use parking lot?

_____ Valets – included? Is there a preferred valet company?

_____ Buses – if using buses - is there room to turn around, unload?

Shipments

_____ Will the venue accept and store boxes a few days before event? $?

Audiovisual Team

_____ Exclusive AV Company?

_____ What tech operators are included, if any? (lighting tech, sound,   camera)

_____ Cost of in-house AV Team/hour/operator

_____ What AV exists in house? See the quality of the projector and check compatibility.

_____ Internet Access- speed and logistics (do you need to drop lines, $$$)

_____ Cost to use existing Internet lines

Stages

_____ Note any restrictions and size dimensions

_____ Height from ground to hang points

_____ See stage lighting with the room dark

_____ Existing backdrops, can you utilize these for event?

_____ If a stage must be brought in understand load-in logistics/restrictions

Registration/Place card area

_____ Is there a clean, open space near entrance of venue and in front of main room?

_____ How much signage can be placed outside of meeting room, in common areas?

_____ Will other events be held during meeting/wedding/party?

_____ Does venue have staff to help with registration/guiding guests to room?

Entrance

_____ Opportunity to brand/decorate entrance area?

_____ Curb appeal; are you comfortable with the current look/feel of the entrance?

Reception Area

_____ How close is the area to the ceremony/meeting room?

_____ Ideally a large open space with the ability to brand/decorate

_____ What furniture can be utilized for event?

_____ Will venue take away existing furniture you don't want for your   event?

Any charges?

_____ How early can you set up in this area?

Other Clients

_____ Who else has held events at this venue in recent months?

_____ Testimonials? Can you contact references?

_____ Has a major competitor hosted parties at this venue for a similar client base?

Electronic versions of this tool with room for notes are available upon request at **products@newbizplaybook.com**.

Food and Beverage Planning

Appetizers

As you determine the appetizer quantity, consider what purpose the appetizers will serve. If you're serving appetizers before a main meal, you don't need as many as you do if the appetizers are the meal itself. Because appetizers are different from other food items, how much you need depends on several factors. Appetizers don't lend themselves to a quantity chart, per se, but let the following list guide you:

- For appetizers preceding a full meal, you should have at least four different types of appetizers and six to eight pieces (total) per person. For example, say you have 20 guests. In that case, you'd need at least 120 total appetizer pieces.

- For appetizers without a meal, you should have at least six different types of appetizers. You should also have 12 to 15 pieces (total) per person. For example, if you have 20 guests, you need at least 240 total appetizer pieces. This estimate is for a three-hour party. Longer parties require more appetizers.

- The more variety you have, the smaller portion size each type of appetizer will need to have. Therefore, you don't need to make as much of any one particular appetizer.

- When you serve appetizers to a crowd, always include bulk-type appetizers. Bulk-type foods are items that aren't individually made, such as dips or spreads. If you forgo the dips and spreads, you'll end up making hundreds of individual appetizer items, which may push you over the edge. To calculate bulk items, assume 1 ounce equals 1 piece.

- Always try to have extra items, such as black and green olives and nuts, for extra filler.

When appetizers precede the meal, you should serve dinner within an hour. If more than an hour will pass before the meal, then you need to increase the number of appetizers. Once again, always err on the side of having too much rather than too little.

Quantity planning for soups, sides, main courses, and desserts

The following tables can help you determine how much food you need for some typical soups, sides, main courses, and desserts. If the item you're serving isn't listed here, you can probably find an item in the same food group to guide you.

You may notice a bit of a discrepancy between the serving per person and the crowd servings. The per-person serving is based on a plated affair (where someone else has placed the food on the plates and the plates are served to the guests). In contrast, buffet-style affairs typically figure at a lower serving per person because buffets typically feature more side dish items than a plated meal does. Don't use the quantity tables as an exact science; use them to guide you and help you make decisions for your particular crowd. If you're serving a dish that you know everyone loves, then make more than the table suggests. If you have a dish that isn't as popular, you can get by with less.

Soups and Stews

Soup or Stew	Per Person	Crowd of 25	Crowd of 50
Served as a first course	1 cup	5 quarts	2-1/2 gallons
Served as an entree	1-1/2 to 2 cups	2 to 2-1/2 gallons	4 gallons

Main Courses

Entree	Per Person	Crowd of 25	Crowd of 50
Baby-back ribs, pork spareribs, beef short ribs	1 pound	25 pounds	50 pounds
Casserole	N/A	Two or three 9-x-13-inch casseroles	Four or five 9-x-13-inch casseroles
Chicken, turkey, or duck (boneless)	1/2 pound	13 pounds	25 pounds
Chicken or turkey (with bones)	3/4 to 1 pound	19 pounds	38 pounds
Chili, stew, stroganoff, and other chopped meats	5 to 6 ounces	8 pounds	15 pounds

	Per Person	Crowd of 25	Crowd of 50
Ground beef	1/2 pound	13 pounds	25 pounds
Maine lobster (about 2 lbs. each)	1	25	50
Oysters, clams, and mussels (medium to large)	6 to 10 pieces	100 to 160 pieces	200 to 260 pieces
Pasta	4 to 5 ounces	7 pounds	16 pounds
Pork	14 ounces	22 pounds	44 pounds
Roast (with bone)	14 to 16 ounces	22 to 25 pounds	47 to 50 pounds
Roast cuts (boneless)	1/2 pound	13 pounds	25 pounds
Shrimp (large: 16 to 20 per pound)	5 to 7 shrimp	7 pounds	14 pounds
Steak cuts (T-bone, porterhouse, rib-eye)	16 to 24 ounces	16 to 24 ounces per person	16 to 24 ounces per person
Turkey (whole)	1 pound	25 pounds	50 pounds

Side Dishes

Side Dish	Per Person	Crowd of 25	Crowd of 50

Asparagus, carrots, cauliflower, broccoli, green beans, corn kernels, peas, black-eyed peas, and so on	3 to 4 ounces	4 pounds	8 pounds
Corn on the cob (broken in halves when serving buffet-style)	1 ear	20 ears	45 ears
Pasta (cooked)	2 to 3 ounces	3-1/2 pounds	7 pounds
Potatoes and yams	1 (medium)	6 pounds	12 pounds
Rice and grains (cooked)	1-1/2 ounces	2-1/2 pounds	5 pounds

Side Salads

Ingredient	Per Person	Crowd of 25	Crowd of 50
Croutons (medium size)	N/A	2 cups	4 cups
Dressing (served on the side)	N/A	4 cups	8 cups
Fruit salad	N/A	3 quarts	6 quarts
Lettuce (iceberg or romaine)	N/A	4 heads	8 heads
Lettuce (butter or red leaf)	N/A	6 heads	12 heads

Potato or macaroni salad	N/A	8 pounds	16 pounds
Shredded cabbage for coleslaw	N/A	6 to 8 cups (about 1 large head of cabbage)	12 to 16 cups (about 2 large heads of cabbage)
Vegetables (such as tomato and cucumber)	N/A	3 cups	6 cups

Breads

Bread	Per Person	Crowd of 25	Crowd of 50
Croissants or muffins	1-1/2 per person	3-1/2 dozen	7 dozen
Dinner rolls	1-1/2 per person	3-1/2 dozen	7 dozen
French or Italian bread	N/A	Two 18-inch loaves	Four 18-inch loaves

Desserts

Dessert	Per Person	Crowd of 25	Crowd of 50
Brownies or bars	1 to 2 per person	2-1/2 to 3 dozen	5-1/2 to 6 dozen
Cheesecake	2-inch	Two 9-inch	Four 9-inch

	wedge	cheesecakes	cheesecakes
Cobbler	1 cup	Two 9-x-9-x-2-inch pans	Four 9-x-9-x-2-inch pans
Cookies	2 to 3	3 to 4 dozen	6 to 8 dozen
Ice cream or sorbet	8 ounces	1 gallon	2 gallons
Layered cake or angel food cake	1 slice	Two 8-inch cakes	Four 8-inch cakes
Pie	3-inch wedge	Two or three 9-inch pies	Four or five 9-inch pies
Pudding, trifles, custards, and the like	1 cup	1 gallon	2 gallons
Sheet cake	2-x-2-inch piece	1/4 sheet cake	1/2 sheet cake

Alcohol and Beverage Planning

It is your choice as to whether to allow alcohol to be served at your event, but you will want to make sure that your venue has a license, or arrangements in place to allow you to serve, should you decide to do so.

Concerning drinks, let the following list guide you:

> Soft drinks: One to two 8-ounce servings per person per hour.

> Punch: One to two 4-ounce servings per person per hour.

> Tea: One to two 8-ounce servings per person per hour.

> Coffee: One to two 4-ounce servings per person per hour.

> Water: Always provide it. Two standard serving pitchers per table are usually enough.

> Again, err on the side of having too much. If people are eating a lot and having fun, they tend to consume more liquid.

Alcohol Consumption and Pricing Projection Tool

There is always some subjectivity in alcohol planning. The assumption here is that 75% of the guests are drinking alcohol. This should be discussed, as a higher percentage of children in attendance, a group of heavier drinkers etc., could impact these assumptions.

As always we recommend adding 10% to all estimates. You will frustrate guests if there is insufficient alcohol, so make sure they are in agreement with your assumptions on numbers. They will know their guests better than anyone. The cost estimates assume average costs on beer, wine, and liquor. Premium beer, wine, and liquor would also mean increased costs. This also assumes equal consumption i.e. 25% each of beer, wine, and liquor. Beer drinkers tend to range closer to 40%, but these figures make scaling for your needs much easier.

The following should help plan for reception alcohol consumption. BD = beer drinker, WD = wine drinker, LD = liquor drinker

	Small Wedding (100 guests)	
	Amount	Cost
Beer	5 cases per 25 BD	75.00
Wine	20 bottles per 25 WD	160.00
Liquor	6 750 ml bottles per 25 LD	90.00

	Medium Wedding (200 guests)	
	Amount	Cost
Beer	9 cases per 50 BD	135.00
Wine	40 bottles per 50 WD	320.00
Liquor	12 750 ml bottles per 50 LD	180.00

	Large Wedding (100)	
	Amount	Cost
Beer	3 Kegs 100 BD	270.00
Wine	79 bottles per 100 WD	632.00
Liquor	24 750 ml bottles per 100 LD	360.00

Seating Planning Tool

Banquet Table

Table Size	Seating Capacity	Linen Size	Space Needed
6'	6-8	90" x 132"	11" x 7"
8'	8-10	90" x 156"	13' x 7'
Classroom 6'	4	70" x 170"	11' x 6'
Classroom 8'	6	70" x 170"	13' x 6'

Round Table

Table Size	Seating Capacity	Linen Size	Space Needed
2.5'	2-4	96" round	7' diameter
3'	4-5	96" round	8' diameter
4'	6-8	108" round	9' diameter
5'	8-10	120" round	10' diameter
6'	10-12	132" round	11' diameter

Cocktail Table

Table Size	Seating Capacity	Linen Size	Space Needed
2.5'	2-4	108" round	7' diameter
3'	4-5	120" round	8' diameter

Dance Floor Planning Tool

This tool has been designed to allow you to plan and scale necessary floor space for dancing. For parties greater than 250, simply use multiples of the tables below. If more than 50% of guests are expected to be dancing, ignore the guests invited column, and plan based upon the number of dancers in the second column.

Total Guests	Dancers	Dance FL Size	Floor SQ Feet
24	12	8'x8'	64
36	18	8'x12'	96
48	24	8'x16'	128
64	32	12'x12'	144
72	36	12'x16'	192
90	45	12'x20	240
96	48	16'x16'	256
120	60	16'x24'	384
128	64	16'x24'	384
144	72	16'x24'	384
150	75	20'x20'	400
168	84	16'x28'	448
180	90	20'x24'	480
192	96	16'x32'	512
210	105	20'x28'	560
250	125	24'x28'	672

Guest List Management Tool

This tool is most easily used in spreadsheet form. An excel file tool is available at newbizplaybook.com. For those who want to download it.

With proper planning, a fair amount of information is needed on each guest including:

1. First and last name

2. Telephone number

3. Address and/or email address

4. Invitation sent

5. Confirmed for attending/or not

6. Confirmed for attending pre-wedding dinner/or not – out of town guests for example

7. Bar/Bat Mitzvah gift

8. Thank you letter sent

Download a great tool for helping the Bar/Bat Mitzvah and parents keep track of attendance, and their responsibilities for thank you cards etc. This tool also helps the event planner to track and make adjustments for food, dance etc., in the event that more or fewer guests attend than expected. Electronic versions of this spreadsheet will be sent to readers upon request at **products@newbizplaybook.com.**

Vendor Contact Planning Sheet

Vendor	Business Name	Contact Name	Contact Number	Payment Status
Photographer				
Minister/Rabi				
Bakery				
Bar Tenders				
Wait staff				
Caterer				
Videographer				
D.J.				
Flowers				

Vendor Commitment Sheet

Vendor	Commitment	Arrival Time	Notes -	Gets Meal -
Photographer	8 hours x2			
Minister/Rabi				
Bakery		2.pm		
Bar Tenders				
Wait staff				No
Caterer				
Videographer				
D.J.				
Flowers				

Invoice Template

Your invoice is as much a reflection of your brand as any business card. You want to finish your engagement as professionally as you started it. We have included a template, and an electronic copy is available at **products@newbizplaybook.com**. Your invoice should include all of the following:

[Company Name]

[Company slogan]

[Street Address]
[City, ST ZIP Code]
Phone [Phone] | Fax [Fax]
[Email] | [Website]

TO
[Name]
[Company Name]
[Street Address]
[City, ST ZIP Code]
Phone [Phone] | [Email]

INVOICE

INVOICE # [Invoice No.]
DATE [Date]

FOR [Project or service description]
P.O. # [P.O. #]

Description	Amount

Total

Make all checks payable to [Company Name]
Payment is due within 30 days.
If you have any questions concerning this invoice, contact [Name] | [Phone] | [Email]

THANK YOU FOR YOUR BUSINESS!

Photographer Interview Questions

Attached are some questions to ask when interviewing photographers, but prior to that, you should speak to your client about what they want in terms of Bar/Bat Mitzvah photography both in the deliverable, and with the style of photographer and his interaction with guests at the party. The photographer should be willing to answer these questions and this interview will give you a sense of his or her business temperament. Eventually you will have a stable of talented vendors who can help you here based on your specific needs, and you may develop special requests that help you make the events you handle unique. *You should also be prepared to provide the photographer with any needed information such as divorced guests, who do not wish to be photographed together etc.

1. Do you have my date available?

2. Do you have an online portfolio that I, and/or my client can review to get a sense of your style, and how recent is the material on it?

3. How far in advance do I need to book with you?

4. How long have you been in business/How many Bar/Bat Mitzvah's have you shot?

5. Are there references you can offer from prior clients or planners? Note: This is the important question in the interview. Do not hire someone who cannot provide you this information, and call at least a couple of the references to compare their answers to your photographer's responses to these questions.

6. How would you describe your photography style (e.g. traditional, photojournalistic, and creative)?

7. How would you describe your approach to interacting with guests, i.e. blending in, stirring the pot for creative photos, choreographing shots?

8. What type of equipment do you use?

9. Are you shooting in digital or film format or both?

10. Do you shoot in color and black & white?

11. Can I give you a list of specific shots we would like?

12. How will you (and your assistants) be dressed?

13. Is it okay if other people take photos while you're taking photos?

14. Have you ever shot at my venue? If not, would you be willing to visit in advance to plan?

15. What time will you arrive at the site and for how long will you shoot?

16. If my event lasts longer than expected, will you stay? Is there an additional charge?

17. Can you put together a slideshow of the Bar/Bat Mitzvah with provided photos and/or a real time slide show for viewing at the reception?

18. What information do you need from me before the event day?

19. What is your rate, and how is ownership of the photos handled? Parents may want to own the photos to copy and use as they see fit, and this may impact price.

20. Are you the photographer who will shoot my event? If not, who will shoot it, and can I see their work? If so, who will be assisting you and how?

21. What are your travel charges/requirements if any?

22. Are you photographing other events on the same day as this event?

23. What type of album designs do you offer? Do you provide any assistance in creating an album?

24. Do you provide retouching, color adjustment or other corrective services?

25. How long after the event will I get the proofs? Will they be viewable online? On a CD?

26. What is the ordering process?

27. How long after I order my photos/album will I get them?

28. Will you give me the negatives or the digital images, and is there a fee for that?

29. When will I receive a written contract?

30. What is your refund/cancellation policy? Do you have someone who covers your events in case of emergency or equipment failure?

Florist Interview Questions

1. Do you have my date available?

2. Do you have an online portfolio that I, and/or my client can review to get a sense of your style, and how recent is the material on it?

3. How far in advance do I need to book with you?

4. How long have you been in business/How many Bar/Bat Mitzvah's have you handled?

5. Are there references you can offer from prior clients or planners? Note: This is the important question in the interview. Do not hire someone who cannot provide you this information, and call at least a couple of the references to compare their answers to your florists responses to these questions.

6. Given the size of this event, flower preference, color scheme, and venue specifics for Synagogue/Temple and reception, what would you propose? Note: Do not lead with your budget. Advise that you are open and want to see the proposal for a few different packages, so that you can compare costs.

7. What time will you arrive at the site and how long will it take you to set up?

8. Who will be managing the setup?

9. Are you providing flowers for other events on the same day as this event?

10. Any rental fees for vases or decorations the florist is providing?

11. Any additional labor charges, taxes, or other fee?

12. When will I receive a written contract?

13. What is your refund/cancellation policy? Do you have someone who covers your events in case of emergency? Note: It is common to require a 50% down payment.

DJ Details

What style DJ do you want: Quiet (no interaction during dancing) Moderate (interaction only if necessary) Outgoing (lots of interaction)

Is it more important for you to hear your favorite music, or for your guests to be dancing? _____

How many crowd-involvement songs would you like played (Electric Slide, Duck Dance, Cha Cha Slide, Cupid Shuffle, Anniversary Dance, etc.)?

These questions asked of your client will help to frame the experience they can expect from their DJ.

Bar/Bat Mitzvah Reception Planning Tool

Contact Information
Client name: Phone/Email:
Bar (boy) / Bat (girl) *(circle one)* Mitzvah name:
Reception Date: Setup Start Time:
Entertainment Start Time: End Time:

The following is a typical but optional sequence of events. The specifics should be coordinated with relevant venders such as caterers, and DJ's etc.

Sequence	Time	Event
		Guests Arrive
		Cocktail Hour
		Main Reception Starts (guests join each other in main hall)
		Family Entrance
		Candle Lighting
		Hora
		Kiddush
		Motzi
		Toasts
		Salad within 30 minutes of entrance
		Guest of Honor/Parent Dance
		Main Course
		Host/Hostess Dance
		Dessert
		Open Dancing
		Finale

Venue Information

There are other tools in this publication for helping you to interview, plan for, and qualify the venue for your event. Those may be used here, so for example, there is a guest tracker in the wedding section. You may want to use something different for this event, but that will work here.

Name/address of establishment:

Contact name: Phone:

Primary room name/location:

Planning Logistics

Number of guests: Children:

Day School Guest of Honor attends: Hebrew School Guest of Honor attends:

Party Theme:

Number of courses to be served (including dessert):

Will the caterer be using the dance floor for a buffet during the cocktail hour?   During the main course?

Contact Information for Other Party Professionals

	Name	Phone	email	Booked From_ to _
Caterer	Grande Dining Cuisine	(123)456-789	abc@def.com	7-9:30
Banquet Hall/Venue				
Planner/Coordinator				
Photographer				
Videographer				
Entertainer				

Cocktail Hour Planning Tool

Is cocktail hour in same room as main reception?   If not, what room is it in?

Music for cocktail hour:
Reception Start (Guests enter main reception room from cocktail room)

Music to start with (high-energy dance music recommended):

Reception Grand Entrance / Introductions

Who will be performing the introductions?

Suggested order of introductions:

1. Parents (usually introduced as Host and Hostess, Bob and Jane)

2. Siblings

3. Guest of Honor

Re songs requested, if not review DJ reference tool for a feel about requests on music options, and DJ style preferences.

Please list those to be introduced during the grand entrance in the order they will be introduced. You can choose different songs for each person or one for the entire group. Use additional sheets if necessary. If you want, interesting tidbits of information about relationships to the guest of honor can be announced—if so, please write details below each person's name.

For each name collect:

Name(s)

Phonetic Pronunciation(s)

How to Introduce

Music

Candle lighting

A memory candle for deceased relative(s) may be lit by the guest of honor. Typically this is announced by the Guest of Honor, and is done either before the first candle is announced, or before the parents' candle is announced. Alternatively, one of the candles on the cake can be lit as a memory candle—this would be announced at the time of that candle. Will there be a memory candle?

Include the names of people who will be coming to the cake. Write the names as the Guest of Honor calls them and include phonetic pronunciation. The usual order for candle lighting is

1.   Grandparents
2.   Aunts
3.   Uncles
4.   Cousins
5.   Older relatives
6.   Younger relatives
7.   Friends of parents
8.   Friends of Guest of Honor
9.   Parents
10.   Siblings
11.   Guest of Honor

The usual number of candles is 14 *(13 for age, one for good luck)*. Try to group relatives and friends together to keep the amount of candles to 14 as best as possible. You can have interesting tidbits of information announced as the individuals come up to light the candles. If you want to do this, please write details below each person's name.

You will also need to choose music to be played while people come up and light the candles. You can have one piece of music serve as background to all of the candles or you may want to match a specific song to each person or group of people lighting the candle (*preferably fun and upbeat*). The total ceremony takes about 15 minutes.

Candle Lighting List

Name(s)	Phonetic Pronunciation(s)	How to Introduce	Music
1.			
2.			
3.			
4.			
5.			
6.			

Events

Hora

Please indicate which family members you would like to be lifted in the chair during the Hora:

Kiddush

Who will be introduced to say the Kiddush blessing? Write the name as the Guest of Honor would, and include phonetic pronunciation.
Motzi

Who will be introduced to say the Motzi blessing? Write the name as the Guest of Honor would, and include phonetic pronunciation.

Toast

Who will be introduced to offer the toast to the Guest of Honor? Typically this is the father. Write the name as the Guest of Honor would, and include phonetic pronunciation.
Will there be other people offering toasts? If so, describe:

After the toast, will the Guest of Honor want to say something? This is a wonderful opportunity to welcome everyone and to do any special acknowledgements, such as guests who have traveled a long distance or friends or family who have contributed in the preparation of the ceremony or reception. This is a fun and memorable alternative to the typical, time-consuming receiving line.

Host/Hostess Dance

Song for host/hostess dance:
You can have us invite your guests to join in partway through the above song, or we can invite them up when the next song begins. When do you want us to invite other guests to join in?

Guest of Honor/Parent Dance

Song for guest of honor/parent dance (we recommend a slow song, some suggestions follow):

After which course (typically after main course):
You can have us invite your guests to join in partway through the above song, or we can invite them up when the next song begins. We can have all fathers/daughters and mothers/sons join you first and invite the rest of the guests to join in one verse later, or we can invite all of the guests to join in at the same time. When and how do you want us to invite other guests to join in?

For some people, a special dance with a Stepfather, Uncle, Brother, or close family friend is done in lieu of, or in addition to, a parents dance.

Grand Finale

Before the last dance, we can organize guests into a circle around the guest of honor, pass the mic around, and allow them to each offer best wishes. Do you want to do this?

Table Photos/Interviews

Please indicate the points (if any) during the reception when you and your photographer want everyone to remain seated for table photos:

Please indicate the points (if any) during the reception when you and your videographer want everyone to remain seated for table interviews:

If the photographer or videographer requests it, do you want us to clear the dance floor or delay the start of dancing for the completion of table photos and/or interviews?

Additional setups require:
Dedications, Birthdays, Anniversaries, Other Special Dances, etc.
List any special announcements you would like us to make. This is a great way to personalize your event and recognize someone special.

Additional Notes *(Use back or additional sheets if necessary)*
If there is anything else we need to know to ensure your reception flows smoothly, please list the details here. In particular:

- If you feel we need to be aware of Any sensitive information regarding your event, family, or guests
- If you are having a video presentation, a singer, musicians, fraternity/sorority serenade, centerpiece giveaway, or any other personalized additions that will make your party unique

Bar/Bat Mitzvah Gift Ideas

(Be sure to send the gift before you go to the event because it
will take place on Shabbat)

1. Siddur (prayer book)
2. Chumash (Bible)
3. Shabbat Candlesticks
4. Silver Kiddush cup,
5. Yad (pointer used during Torah reading)
6. Havdalah Set
7. Tzedakah (box for charity to encourage giving)
8. Nice watch
9. Hamsa charms
10. Star of David, Chai, or Religiously themed jewelry
11. Wool Bnei or Tallit
12. Cash or gift certificates in increments of 18

Bar/Bat Mitzvah Theme Ideas

Bat Mitzvah Ideas

1. Fashion/Runway Themes
2. Technology or Music Themes
3. Candy or Chocolate Themes
4. Exotic City Themes (Paris for example)
5. Movie Themes
6. Sports Themes
7. Bling or Bedazzle Themes
8. Teen Lounge/Dance Themes
9. Gymnastic Themes
10. Hollywood Themes

Bar Mitzvah Ideas

1. Action and Super Heroes
2. Technology or Music Themes
3. Sports Themes
4. Car/Racing/Monster Truck Themes
5. Arcade or Gaming Themes
6. Graffiti Wall Themes
7. Futuristic Themes
8. Teen Lounge/Dance Themes
9. Space Themes
10. Medieval Fantasy Themes